Contents

Between land and sea

Coasts are places where land masses border seas or large lakes. Because tides, waves and sea currents constantly change the actual border between land and water, coasts are zones rather than boundary lines. They include the sea-shore and areas that are affected by salty sea water or wind-blown spray, such as cliffs, sand dunes, marshes or swamps.

The shallow offshore waters around coasts cover gently sloping continental shelves. These shelves are really part of the continents, the higher sections of which form islands, such as the British Isles and Newfoundland. The oceans proper start at the edge of the continental shelves, where there are steep slopes that plunge down to the dark ocean depths.

Coasts are fascinating places. Each shore has its own special character and wildlife, be it rock, sand, mud or shingle. The climate also affects the nature of coasts. In polar regions, many coastlands are buried beneath thick ice sheets that sometimes extend far out to sea as floating ice shelves. In the tropics, by contrast, many coasts are lined by jagged coral reefs which teem with colourful marine life.

Prehistoric people were attracted to coastlands, because food was readily available there. Even today, coasts and the fertile plains behind them support some of the world's largest populations. Many great cities, such as Shanghai, Tokyo, New York City and Sydney, are seaports, while others, including London and Paris, lie not far from the sea on navigable rivers.

Until the early nineteenth century, coastal shipping was the cheapest form of transport in many countries. Although coastal traffic has declined because of competition with railways and roads, trade remains a major activity on coasts. Fishing, tourism and, in some areas, mining, are other leading occupations for coastal peoples.

Glaciers reach the shore along the coast of Greenland, which contains the world's second largest ice sheet.

This book is to be returned on or before
the last date stamped below.

551.45

14 JUL 1997

LIBREX

LYE KEITH

Coasts.

Our World

COASTS

Keith Lye

Titles in this series

Coasts	Mountains
Deserts	Polar Regions
The Earth in Space	Rivers and Lakes
Grasslands	Seas and Oceans
Jungles and Rainforests	Temperate Forests

First published in 1987 by
Wayland (Publishers) Ltd
61 Western Road, Hove
East Sussex BN3 1JD England

© Copyright 1987 Wayland (Publishers) Ltd

Edited by Susannah Foreman

Designed by David Armitage

British Library Cataloguing in Publication Data:
Lye, Keith
 Coasts.—(Our world).
 1. Coasts—Juvenile literature
 I. Title II. Series
 551.4′57   GB451.2
 ISBN 1–85210–037–0

Typeset by DP Press, Sevenoaks, Kent
Printed in Italy by G. Canale & C.S.p.A., Turin
Bound in Belgium by Casterman S.A.

Front cover, main picture Coastal erosion near Hartland Point, Devon, England.
Front cover, inset The sea otter.
Back cover Sunset over the Galapagos Islands.

Left Waves batter the hard limestone cliffs in Dyfed, in south-western Wales. As the cliffs recede, blocks of limestone are left isolated as sea stacks.

Below Sydney, Australia, stands on one of the world's most beautiful natural harbours. Founded in 1788, Sydney is now Australia's busiest seaport.

Changing coasts

Sea water is constantly moving and, as it moves, it changes the shape of coastlines. The most obvious changes in water level are caused by the daily tides. The tidal range in coastal waters may be 6 metres or more, particularly if the water is funnelled in bays or narrow river estuaries. However, the tidal range is extremely low in enclosed or nearly enclosed seas, such as the Baltic and the Mediterranean.

Tidal and other currents, together with powerful storm waves, erode (wear away) some coasts and build up new land along others. For example, currents and waves have cut back the Holderness coast in eastern England by 3 to 5 km since Roman times.

Other natural forces change coasts. During the Ice Age, which ended only 10,000 years ago, much of the world's water was frozen in ice sheets and the sea level was around 120 metres or so lower than today. The British Isles were then linked to mainland Europe. Siberia was joined to Alaska, and a waterway little wider than the modern English Channel separated Asia from Australia. When the ice melted, the sea level rose, changing the shapes of coastlines. One result was that the British Isles were cut off from Europe in about 5500 BC.

The sea level is still rising today by around 30 cm every hundred years. This is caused mainly by polar ice melting. However, earth movements also depress or raise the land. Subsiding coasts often contain deep inlets which were once valleys. Flooded river valleys are called rias and flooded glacial valleys are called fjords. Rising coasts are often marked by raised beaches (wave-cut platforms), which lie well above the level of the highest tides.

Below Tides: The effect of the moon's gravitational pull on the sea.

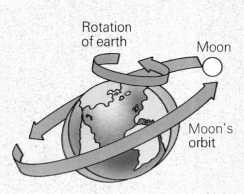

Tides are rises and falls in sea level. They occur twice every 24 hours and 50 minutes. Tides are caused by the gravitational pull of the moon and, to a lesser extent, the sun on the ocean water. When the moon is overhead, water is pulled towards it. There is a similar bulge on the opposite side of the earth, because there the moon's pull is greater on the hard crust than on the oceans. The bulges move around the earth, causing tides, as the earth spins on its axis. The moon also moves forwards on its orbit. As a result, it takes 24 hours and 50 minutes – not 24 hours – for the moon to be overhead at any point on the earth.

Rotation of earth

Moon

Moon's orbit

The highest tidal range (the difference between high and low tide level) occurs when the sun, moon and earth are in a straight line, because the gravitational pull of the sun and moon are then combined. These so-called spring-tides occur at full and new moon. The lowest tidal ranges occur when the sun, earth and moon form a right angle. These are the neap-tides. The highest of all tidal ranges occur at the equinoxes – March 21 and September 21 – when the sun, moon and earth come closest to forming a perfect straight line. These are called the equinoctial spring-tides.

Above In the Ice Age, the coast of south-western New Zealand was much like polar regions today. Glaciers carved deep valleys. When the ice melted, the sea level rose. The drowned glacial valleys are called fjords.

Spring-tides

Sun Moon Earth

Neap-tides

Sun Earth Moon

Above Coastal erosion is fastest where the rocks are soft, such as on the Isle of Sheppey, in the Thames estuary, where London Clay covers the land.

Receding coasts

On calm days, beaches are peaceful places. But after a storm, coastal roads well above high tide level are often littered with pebbles and small rocks, thrown there by powerful storm waves. This action, called corrasion, is one of the ways in which waves make coasts recede. Loose rocks hurled at the bottoms of cliffs by waves hollow out caves. The process gradually undermines the cliffs and, periodically, slabs of overlying rock come crashing down, making the cliff retreat.

The sea erodes coasts in three other ways. Firstly, hydraulic action occurs when waves batter against cliff faces, trapping air in crevices. When the pressure is released, the compressed air in the crevices expands with explosive force, enlarging the crevices and cracks by breaking up the rock. Secondly, corrosion, or chemical action, takes place when sea water dissolves such rocks as limestone. Thirdly, through attrition, loose rocks are ground against each other, turning them into finer and finer particles.

Relatively soft rocks, such as shale or moraine (loose deposits dumped by glaciers at the end of the Ice Age), and rocks soluble in sea water are eroded at a faster rate than hard, compact rocks, such as basalt or sandstone. Wave action erodes outcrops

Pulpit Rock, off the coast of Portland in southern England, is a limestone stack cut off by wave erosion. It can be reached by a jetty.

Above This natural arch has been hollowed out in layers of volcanic rock by the restless waves of the Indian Ocean, at Shimoni in south-eastern Kenya.

of these less resistant rocks to form bays and coves, while harder rocks often remain as headlands. But even rocky headlands are eventually removed. What often happens is that waves attack both sides of a headland, wearing out caves. These caves meet to form natural arches. Eventually, the arches collapse and all that remains of the seaward end of the rocky headland is an isolated pillar of rock called a stack.

Right Wave erosion gradually wears out caves in headlands made of hard rock. When the roof of a cave collapses, a blow-hole appears on the surface. Eventually, caves on opposite sides of a headland meet to form a natural arch. When the arch collapses, a stack is all that remains of the headland.

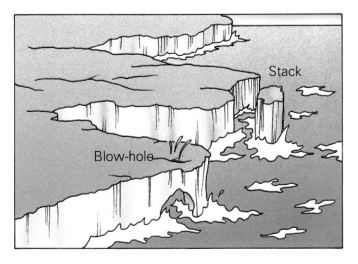

Advancing coastlines

Erosion of coasts produces a great deal of loose, rocky material. This is supplemented by silt carried by rivers. Some of this is swept out to sea, while other material is moved along the shore. The way in which this material is carried along the coast is called longshore drift. The zig-zag movement occurs because waves (the swash) usually rush up beaches at an oblique angle to the shore, pushing loose material upwards. Then the backwash flows directly down the slope, dragging the loose material downwards at right angles to the shore. Sea walls, called groynes, are often built at right angles to the shore to slow down longshore drift and so protect beaches from erosion.

Longshore drift continues unceasingly along straight coasts, but stops where the coast changes direction, as at headlands. Here the sand and pebbles are often deposited in low ridges, called spits. Many spits are curved, because waves deflect the material towards the shore.

Left This aerial view shows a sand bar at Cape Hatteras in North Carolina, in the USA. The map (below) shows the offshore bars and spits in this region. They protect the sounds (or lagoons) and coastal swamps from the fury of Atlantic storm waves.

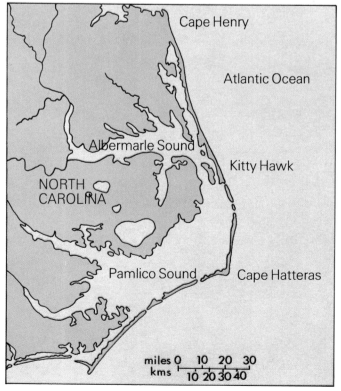

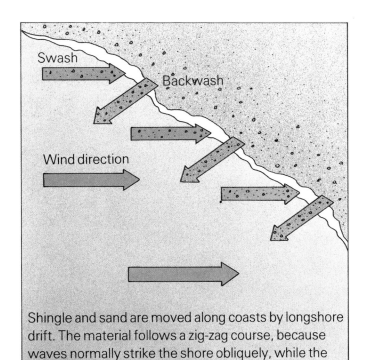

Shingle and sand are moved along coasts by longshore drift. The material follows a zig-zag course, because waves normally strike the shore obliquely, while the backwash is always at right angles to the shore.

Some spits extend from one headland to another and they may eventually seal off bays from the sea. Lakes, or lagoons, formed behind such spits gradually fill up with silt. First they become marshes and then later dry land. A spit which forms a natural bridge between the mainland and an island is known by an Italian term, a tombolo. Similar to spits are bars, which are low ridges of sand and pebbles that pile up offshore, often parallel to the coast. Some form barrier islands.

Coasts advance in other ways. In volcanic areas, streams of molten lava often reach the sea, forming high cliffs when they cool and solidify. At river mouths where the offshore currents are weak, river silt piles up to form flat areas known as deltas.

Below One of nature's most awesome spectacles occurs when streams of molten lava reach the sea, pushing the shoreline farther out. It can sometimes be seen on the coast of the volcanic island of Iceland.

Coral coasts

Above Coral polyps live in warm, shallow seas. They secrete stony external skeletons, which build up into thick layers of limestone.

Marine organisms, called coral polyps, can also play a part in creating coasts. Polyps are small, jelly-like creatures related to sea anemones. They extract calcium carbonate from sea water and secrete it around the lower parts of their bodies to form hard external skeletons. Polyps live in vast colonies. They build their external skeletons on top of the lifeless ones below and so they gradually build up thick layers of calcium carbonate, which form limestone.

Low, circular or horseshoe-shaped coral islands are called atolls. They sometimes surround a central lagoon. Coral ridges, or reefs, include fringing reefs which extend outwards from the shore. By contrast, barrier reefs lie offshore, though they usually follow the same general shape as the coast. The largest coral formation in the world is the Great Barrier Reef off Queensland, in north-east Australia. About 2,200 km long, it has an area of about 207,000 sq km.

Most living coral is in tropical regions, because polyps can live only in warm water between about 20°C and 30°C. The water must also be clear, because polyps cannot live in water clouded by sediment. Polyps also require sunlight and do not survive at depths of more than about 50 metres. Yet the coral in some atolls is 1,000 metres or more thick. These islands probably began as reefs in the shallow waters around isolated volcanic islands. Then the sea level rose as the ice sheets melted at the end of the Ice Age, or perhaps earth movements caused the islands to sink. Whatever the reason, the coral growth must have kept pace with the gradual changes. Otherwise, the great thicknesses of limestone could not have been created.

Right The Great Barrier Reef off north-eastern Australia is the world's largest coral formation.

The Great Barrier Reef has formed on a downfaulted block of land off the coast of Queensland. The higher parts of the block form islands. But most of the islands are made of coral. There are two main types of coral reefs. Fringing reefs form along the shore. Barrier reefs form in shallow offshore waters. Some are close to land, such as Australia's Inner Barrier Reef. Some, such as the Great Barrier Reef itself, are farther out.

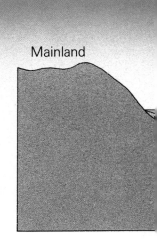

Mainland

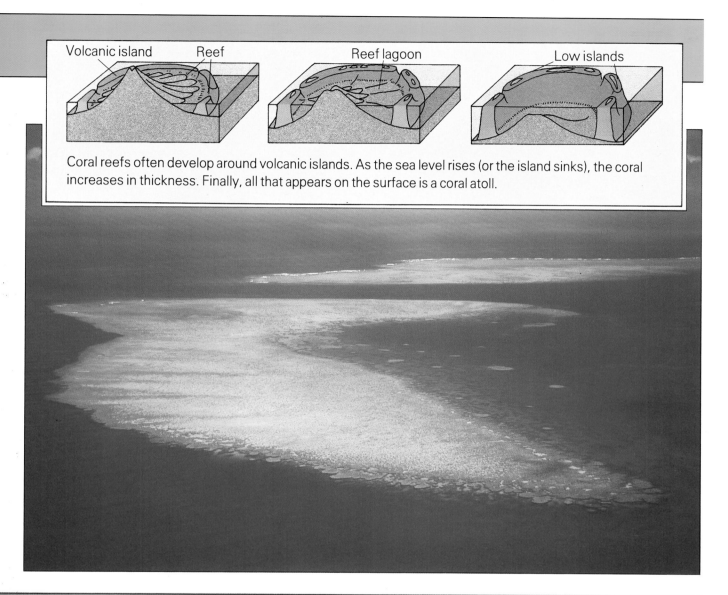

Volcanic island   Reef   Reef lagoon   Low islands

Coral reefs often develop around volcanic islands. As the sea level rises (or the island sinks), the coral increases in thickness. Finally, all that appears on the surface is a coral atoll.

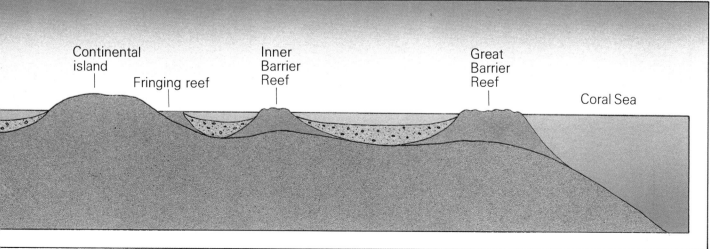

Continental island
    Fringing reef
                        Inner
                        Barrier
                        Reef
                                            Great
                                            Barrier
                                            Reef
                                                        Coral Sea

Land and water

Coasts have distinctive climates. Although both land and sea receive the same amount of sunlight, the land heats up and cools down faster than the sea. This causes sea breezes. For example, by day, the land warms quickly and heats the air, which expands and rises. Cool air from the sea is then sucked in to replace it. At night, the sea is relatively warmer than the land and air flows from the land towards the sea. Sea breezes generally give coasts a milder climate than places inland. This is also the case in winter, when the water is often warmer than the land. Warm onshore winds raise temperatures along coasts, though they often also bring rain.

Ocean currents affect coastal climates. The Gulf Stream is a warm current that flows from the Gulf of Mexico across the North Atlantic Ocean. This current's northern extension, the North Atlantic Drift, warms the coasts of Scandinavia and the British Isles. As a result, Norwegian ports far to the

Right Winds blow storm clouds from the oceans to the land. This is part of the water cycle, whereby land areas get a regular supply of fresh water.

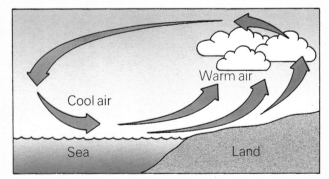

DAY

Warm air

Cool air

Sea   Land

During the day, land heats up more quickly than the sea. Warm air over the land rises and air is drawn in from the sea, creating cool sea breezes.

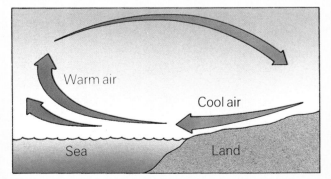

NIGHT

Warm air

Cool air

Sea   Land

At night, the land cools quickly, while the sea retains its heat. As a result, cool air blows from the land to the sea.

north of the Arctic Circle remain ice-free in winter. By contrast, the coasts of eastern Canada far to the south of the Arctic Circle are chilled by the icy Labrador Current. These coasts have much cooler climates than the coasts of northern Norway.

Cold currents affect rainfall. The Peru, or Humboldt, Current flows up the west coasts of Chile and Peru in South America. Onshore winds chilled by this current lower temperatures on land and bring fogs. But as the winds blow inland, the air becomes warmer and tends to pick up moisture. This factor has helped to create the Atacama Desert, one of the world's driest places. And the Benguela Current off south-western Africa has helped to create the bleak Namib Desert.

The northern port of Hammerfest, Norway, is always ice-free because it is warmed by the North Atlantic Drift.

Sand dunes reach the sea in the Namib desert, along the coast of south-western Africa.

Coastal disasters

Most people love the seaside, but living on coasts can be dangerous. High waves caused by storm winds can breach sea walls and cause floods. On 31 January 1953, a severe depression was centred over the North Sea. Wind speeds reaching 185 km/h, combined with a high tide, raised water levels to alarming heights. That night, waves burst through the sea walls along the Dutch coast, flooding 4.3 per cent of the country and killing 1,800 people. There was also severe flooding in eastern Britain. The danger from such storms, combined with the steadily rising sea level, alerted the Dutch and British to strengthen their coastal defences. The Thames Barrier, which was opened in 1984, will prevent tidal surges sweeping up the river and flooding London.

High tidal surges in the Thames River, which occur with storms at spring-tides, now cannot flood central London. When danger threatens, the movable Thames Barrier at Woolwich is closed.

Other destructive storms, called hurricanes, tropical cyclones, typhoons or willy-willies (in Australia) form over the oceans north and south of the equator. These rotating storms are regions of extremely low air pressure and fierce winds, which sometimes reach 300 km/h. They cause much destruction along the coastlands of eastern North America, south-eastern and southern Asia, and northern Australia. In 1979, a hurricane caused damage estimated at $2,300 million in the USA.

Some huge waves along coasts are caused not by winds, but by earthquakes or volcanic eruptions. These waves are called tsunamis, a Japanese term. As these fast-moving waves enter shallow coastal waters, friction makes the water pile up to enormous heights. The highest recorded tsunami was 85 metres high. It appeared off the Japanese Ryukyu Islands.

Storm waves and tsunamis are a danger to shipping. During severe storms, ships may be carried some way inland and stranded on dry land.

Weather forecasters now use photographs taken by space satellites to discover the directions and speeds at which hurricanes are moving across the oceans.

The sea-shore

Naturalists divide coasts into zones. At the top is a splash, or spray, zone, above the highest spring-tide level. An upper zone lies between the highest spring-tide level and the average high tide level. A middle zone is between the average high tide and the average low tide level, while a lower zone is below the average low tide level Seashore plants and animals vary from those that cannot survive long without salt walter, to those species with little tolerance to salt.

The splash zone includes cliff tops, where land plants mingle with those adapted to survive salt from sea spray, such as samphire and sea-rocket. Many rocky cliff faces are bare, but some weathered cliffs may be covered by such attractive plants as thrift (sea pink).

Few plants or animals live on shingle beaches, because the pebbles are constantly churned

Right A root-like holdfast secures this rockweed to the shore, preventing the waves sweeping it away.

Right Rocky beaches have their own special plant and animal communities. The diagram shows some of the living things found on rocky shores bordering the North Atlantic Ocean. Each species must prevent itself being washed around by the waves and damaged. Seaweeds do this with their holdfasts. Such animals as barnacles permanently attach themselves to rocks. Limpets have a powerful foot, which clamps the animal's body to a rock by suction. Other animals shelter in crevices.

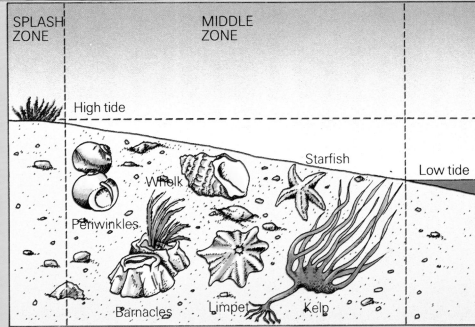

together by wave action. Many sandy and muddy beaches look lifeless, apart from a few grasses, but they are usually the homes of many burrowing animals – invisible at low tide.

Rocky beaches support seaweeds. Seaweeds are algae, lacking roots, stems, leaves, flowers and fruits. Instead, the main part, the frond, is supported by a holdfast (a root-like part), which anchors the plant to a rock. There are three main types of seaweed. Green seaweed tends to be found near the top of rocky shores, brown seaweed in the centre and red seaweed at the bottom.

Animals also show special adaptations. Burrowing animals, such as lugworms, ragworms, razor shells, shrimps, cockles and some crabs, spend much of their lives buried in wet sand or mud Other soft-bodied creatures are protected by tough shells. When the tide falls, some animals seek shelter in crevices, beneath stones or under seaweed. Others, such as barnacles, limpets and mussels, anchor themselves firmly to rocks.

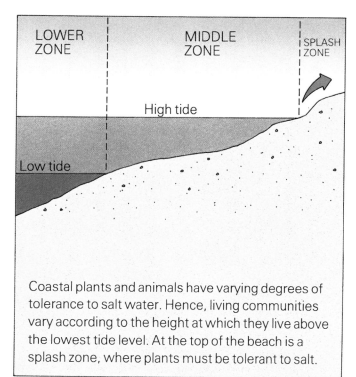

Coastal plants and animals have varying degrees of tolerance to salt water. Hence, living communities vary according to the height at which they live above the lowest tide level. At the top of the beach is a splash zone, where plants must be tolerant to salt.

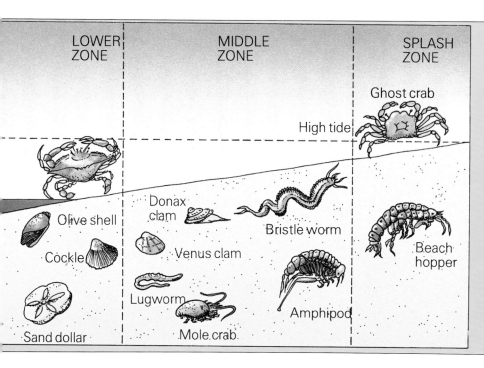

Left The diagram shows some of the species found on sandy beaches in the North Atlantic. Here creatures must protect themselves at low tide. Many are burrowing animals. For example, lugworms live in L-shaped burrows, the open end of which is identifiable because it is often surrounded by worm casts. Sand hoppers live in burrows, while some crabs hide in the sand or mud at low tide and re-emerge to swim at high tide. Other creatures hide under stones or plants.

Dunes and swamps

Other distinctive coastal environments include sand dunes, salt marshes and mangrove swamps.

Many sand dunes lie in the splash zone and so the best adapted plants are halophytes (plants that tolerate salt), such as sea couch grass. To prevent dunes burying farmland, they are often anchored by planting marram grass, whose underground stems grow through the sand. But marram grass cannot grow near high tide level, because it is fairly intolerant of salt. Anchored sand dunes are sometimes turned into golf courses or planted with pine trees.

Salt marshes are generally found in sheltered areas, such as river estuaries, inlets or lagoons that lie behind shingle spits. They are important because many animals lay their eggs in these spots. Salt marsh plants have difficulty in absorbing water, because sea water contains concentrations of mineral salts similar to those in plant cells. Some plants increase the salt in their tissues to concentrations far above that contained in sea water, so that they can continue to draw water from the soil. Others have swollen stems and leaves to store water.

Another problem for plants growing in or near water is a lack of oxygen. Some grasses and rushes have aerial tissue to absorb oxygen, while aerial roots are characteristic of trees in tropical mangrove swamps. The stilt-like roots of mangrove trees serve another purpose. They trap mud brought down by rivers and help to transform these coastal swamps into land areas. Perhaps the best-known inhabitant of mangrove swamps is the mudskipper. This small fish spends as much time out of water as in it. At low tide, it propels itself over the mud with its flippers and fins. Some even climb trees as the tide rises and hang from branches, suspended by a sucker.

Sand dunes are moved around by the wind. Marram grass, whose roots bind the loose sand grains together, is often planted to stabilize the dunes.

Mangrove swamps, which line some tropical coasts, contain specially adapted trees with aerial roots. Animals include burrowing crabs and mudskippers – fish that can walk across the mud.

Life in coastal waters

Shallow coastal waters which receive abundant sunlight are the home of many kinds of living organisms. Firstly, there are free-floating, microscopic plants and animals, called plankton, on which all creatures depend directly or indirectly for food. Major groups of larger creatures include sponges; coelenterates, such as sea anemones and jellyfish; molluscs, including sea snails, squids, octopuses and such bivalves as oysters and mussels; crustaceans, such as crabs, crayfish, lobsters, prawns and shrimps; and echinoderms, including sea-urchins and starfish.

The oceans contain more than 20,000 kinds of fish, more than 95 per cent of which have bony skeletons. Common inshore bony fish include dabs, flounders, John Dories, plaice, mullet and snappers. Some species, such as mackerel, spawn near the shore but migrate to deeper waters in summer.

Some sharks live in coastal waters, while others from the open sea are occasional visitors to coasts. Sharks, together with rays and chimaeras, belong to a group of fish that have skeletons of cartilage rather than bone. Sharks have a fearsome reputation, but the recorded attacks on people number, on average, only about 100 a year throughout the entire world.

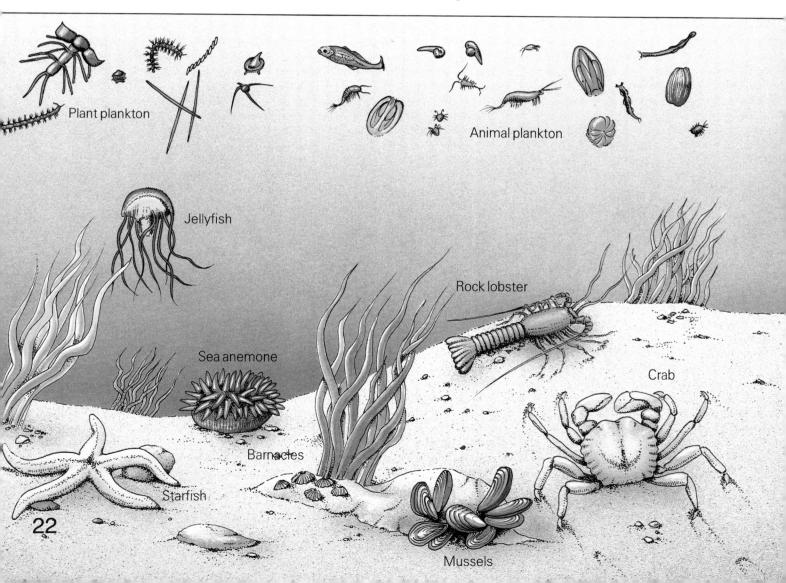

Plant plankton

Animal plankton

Jellyfish

Rock lobster

Sea anemone

Crab

Barnacles

Starfish

Mussels

The colourful world of coral reefs is the home of many exquisite creatures, including angelfish. This Queen Angelfish is found off the San Blas Islands, Panama.

Some of the most varied animal communities are found in coral reefs. More than a third of all salt water fish species live in the coral reefs of the Indian and Pacific Oceans, while many other species inhabit West Indian reefs. Although the coral skeletons are generally white, they are swathed in colourful tissue. Many plants, invertebrates and fish, including the appropriately named angel fish, butterfly fish and parrot fish, are also very colourful. The only drab creatures are predators, such as stone fish, which do not want to draw attention to themselves. Coral reefs are ideal for snorkelling or scuba diving.

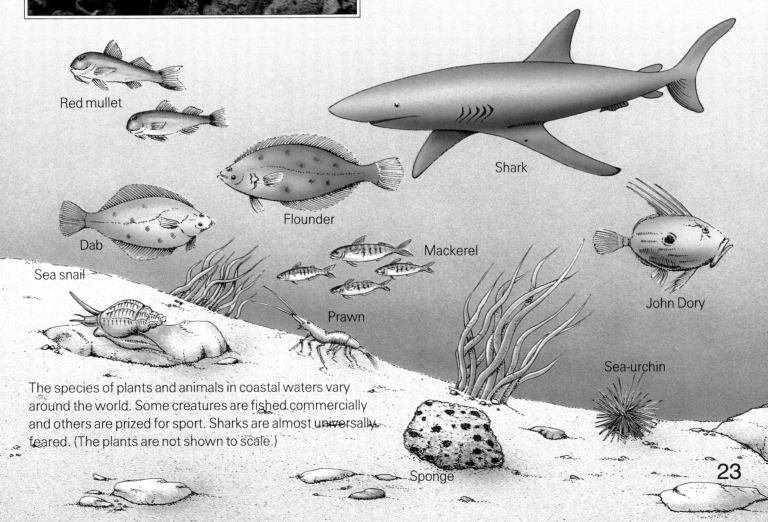

Red mullet

Shark

Flounder

Dab

Mackerel

Sea snail

John Dory

Prawn

Sea-urchin

The species of plants and animals in coastal waters vary around the world. Some creatures are fished commercially and others are prized for sport. Sharks are almost universally feared. (The plants are not shown to scale.)

Sponge

Birds

Of the 8,600 or so species of birds, 285 are classed as sea birds. Some, including albatrosses, petrels, shearwaters and skuas, spend most of their lives at sea, though they return to land to raise their young. There are also inshore sea birds, including many migrants, which nest in polar regions but winter on temperate coasts, and offshore species, which feed in the sea not far from the shore.

Inshore species include most gulls, which are famed scavengers. Related to gulls are skimmers, which scoop up small fish and other prey from surface waters, and terns, which catch fish by diving into the sea from the air. Terns are powerful fliers. Some arctic terns travel about 35,400 km a year between the Arctic Circle and Antarctica. Other inshore migrants are geese, which are often seen on salt marshes or mud flats, and ducks, including pintails and the related wigeons and teals. Cormorants and their relatives, shags, are fine swimmers which use their long, thin beaks to catch fish as they dive underwater. Oystercatchers are long-legged waders, which use their beaks to prise open shellfish. Other waders include avocets, curlews and godwits.

Offshore coastal birds include the flightless penguins. However ungainly they may appear, penguins are superb underwater swimmers, reaching speeds of 40 km/h. Gannets and boobies

Adélie penguins breed on the coasts of Antarctica. Like other penguins, they are strong swimmers and live on fish. In turn, they are preyed on by leopard seals.

Above Bass Rock, an isolated, volcanic island in south-eastern Scotland, is a bird sanctuary, famed for its gannets. About 9,000 pairs nest there.

are spectacular divers. They sometimes plunge vertically about 30 metres from the air into the sea. Other offshore species including auks and frigate birds.

Coastal birds now face increasing hazards. Natural habitats, such as salt marshes and nest sites, are disappearing. Another threat is pollution caused by floating oil slicks, poisonous insecticides and industrial wastes which often reach coasts through rivers (see pages 38–39).

Below Gulls are scavengers, ready at any time to clear up any unwanted scraps of fish.

Mammals and reptiles

A major group of marine mammals, the Pinnepedia, lives mainly in temperate and polar seas. The three main types are eared seals, such as fur seals and sea lions; earless seals, which have small ear openings but no external ears, including elephant seals and harbour seals; and walruses, the only members of this group with tusks.

Seals feed on fish and squid, while walruses eat molluscs and crustaceans. With their sleek, torpedo-shaped bodies, seals are fine swimmers. Many have hair on their bodies and they are all insulated by blubber under the skin. Some seals spend most of their lives in the sea, but all of them breed on land. Sharks, killer whales and polar bears prey on seals, but their chief enemy is the human hunter. One marine mammal in the North Pacific Ocean, the sea otter, was almost hunted to extinction, but is now protected by international agreements.

Whales are occasionally seen near coasts and they are sometimes grounded in shallows. In July 1986, more than eighty false killer whales were stranded on the north coast of Western Australia. Teams of people poured water on the helpless animals and others tried to coax them back into the sea. Eventually, two bull whales were towed out to sea, where their signals lured many of the others back to safety.

Marine reptiles include sea turtles. They live mostly in warm seas, though females return to breeding beaches to lay their eggs. The marine iguanas on the Galapagos Islands are coastal reptiles which feed on seaweed. There are also between 50 and 60 species of venomous sea snakes, mostly in the Indian and Pacific Oceans. As many give birth to live young, they have no need to come on land to lay eggs. They include the Australian Yellow-bellied sea snake and the sea krait.

The sandy beaches of Ascension Island are one of the few breeding sites of green turtles. After laying their eggs, they return to the warm coastal waters of Brazil.

Above The polar bear, found in Arctic regions, is equally at home on land or in the water.

Above The sea otter was hunted almost to extinction, but it can now be seen off the coast of California.

Main picture Cape fur seals bask in the surf off the Atlantic coast of the Namib desert.

Ways of life

From the earliest times, hunting and fishing communities have developed on coasts. Until recently, the Eskimos of the Arctic depended on hunting and fishing, but contact with the outside world has now effectively destroyed their traditional way of life.

After the development of agriculture around 8,000 years ago, farming communities arose inland, and trade developed between coastal peoples and their farming neighbours. Trade is still a vital part of life on coasts. Many peoples along the shores of southern Asia live by fishing and trading. Some, such as the Boat People of Hong Kong, also live on their vessels. In the early years of the Industrial Revolution, coal-fired tramp steamers shipped coastal and international trade, carrying bulky cargoes of mineral ores, timber and grain. Their importance declined when railways were built. But even today, coastal shipping transports more than a tenth of Britain's internal trade.

Much trade is concentrated on large ports, such as Rio de Janeiro, Brazil, and Sydney, Australia, both of which have beautiful, natural harbours. Other ports, such as Takoradi, Ghana, are built on artificial harbours. Many ports have developed into

Lighthouses are built on coasts to give ships warning of dangerous rocks and reefs.

thriving industrial cities, because they can easily import all the raw materials they need.

Because they understand the dangers of the sea, coastal peoples are concerned about the safety of anyone afloat. Around Britain about 130 lifeboats stand ready to go to sea at any time. Most crew members are volunteers.

Other safety precautions along coasts include lighthouses, which inform navigators of dangerous rocks and reefs. However, the importance of lighthouses has declined because of the introduction of electronic navigational systems. Serving a similar function to lighthouses are lightships. These are often positioned near offshore sandbanks, such as the dangerous Goodwin Sands in the English Channel, which is the scene of many shipwrecks.

Below When land is scarce, some coastal people live on boats. The Hong Kong Boat People not only live on their boats, but they also fish and trade in them.

Above The houses in some coastal villages in the Philippines are built on stilts. Fishing boats can be brought right to the front door.

Winning land from the sea

In countries where land is scarce, people have set about turning coastal areas unsuited for agriculture into farmland. This has usually involved a long struggle to push back the shoreline.

The leading experts in reclaiming land from the sea are the Dutch, who have a saying: 'God created the world, but the Dutch created Holland'. Two-fifths of Holland (officially The Netherlands) is below sea level at high tide. Most of this flat land has been reclaimed from the sea.

Land reclamation began about 800 years ago. Sea walls, called dykes, were built around flooded or marshy coastal areas and the water was removed by pumps powered by windmills. These areas, called polders, were then criss-crossed with drainage canals. The rain gradually washed away the salt in the soil, making it fertile. The most ambitious projects have been undertaken in this century, when steam, diesel and electric drainage pumps were available. One was the reclamation of the Zuider Zee. This former bay was first cut off from the sea by the building of a dam nearly 32 km long. The polders behind the dam were then turned partly into farmland and partly into a freshwater lake, IJsselemeer.

Another large project was created in the south-west, where the Maas and Rhine rivers empty into the sea, following the 1953 flood described on page 16. Called the Delta Project, it involved closing sea inlets and reclaiming the land behind them. The final section of the Delta Project was opened in October 1986.

Dutch engineers were also largely responsible in the seventeenth century for land reclamation in areas around the Wash and the mouth of the River Humber in eastern England. They have also applied their experience in South America, notably in Surinam (formerly Dutch Guiana).

Romney Marsh was once a bay of the sea. It later became a marsh, but it has been reclaimed since Roman times. Sea walls hold back the waves.

Above Reclaimed polders in the Netherlands are criss-crossed by drainage canals.

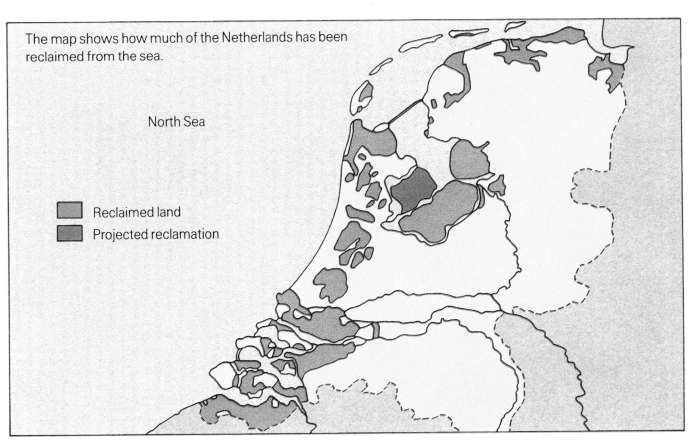

The map shows how much of the Netherlands has been reclaimed from the sea.

North Sea

Reclaimed land
Projected reclamation

The law and fishing

Not long ago, zones between 5 and 10 km beyond coasts were considered to be 'territorial seas'. Beyond them lay the 'high seas', where ships from any country could operate.

However, from the early days of the Industrial Revolution, in the late eighteenth century, trade and fishing increased. Many countries became concerned over the exploitation, particularly the overfishing, of waters outside their territorial seas. Many laws have been proposed to deal with these problems, but agreement has been hard to achieve.

The United Nations has made several proposals, including a 19-km zone where countries can enforce such matters as customs checks. Also proposed is a law giving countries the right to exploit resources, such as oil deposits, beneath the continental shelf, though the outer limit is not precisely defined. A third proposal is the setting up of Exclusive Economic Zones (EEZs), extending 370 km off the coast. Within such zones, countries would have the power to stop overfishing and pollution. Some countries, including Canada, Iceland and the USA, have set up such zones. But other countries still claim historic rights to fish within the EEZs of other countries.

Differences such as these have prevented international agreements on a law of the sea, although many countries have local agreements with others. Obtaining agreement is important, because fish is a major food and, in places, the leading source of protein.

Most of the catch comes from seas over continental shelves, where fish are netted by trawling, seining and drifting, or caught on baited hooks attached to long lines. Many ships now use radar or echo-sounders to locate shoals, while modern factory ships process, package and freeze fish while still at sea.

Many coastal peoples depend entirely on the sea for their livelihood. Checking nets, as here in Indonesia, is a vital operation.

An Australian fisherman loads his boat with pots, which he uses to trap crayfish.

Mining

Coastal waters supply not only food, but also another essential for human health, salt (sodium chloride). Salt is obtained simply by evaporating sea water. Sea water is a complex substance. Besides common salt, it contains many other elements, though most of them occur in such tiny quantities that they are too costly to extract. However, three substances – bromine, iodine and magnesium – are recovered from sea salt.

Other minerals occur in sediments on beaches or on the sea-bed. These minerals are fragments worn from the land and washed into the sea. Sand and gravel used in construction work are obtained by

New techniques have had to be developed to extract oil and natural gas from offshore fields. Drilling rigs must reach high safety standards.

dredging, as are the diamonds found on the coast of southern Namibia. The hard rock beneath the sea-bed can also be mined. Some coal-mines on coasts have shafts that extend under the sea.

Other substances are obtained from bore holes drilled into the sea-bed. Sulphur and potash dissolved in water are pumped up through bore holes. But much more important are oil and natural gas. Offshore drilling is expensive, but the rising demand for oil and gas has led to a great expansion in offshore production. Offshore drilling was at first

Below A stretch of beach 80 km long on the Namibian coast of Africa yields the richest supply of gem diamonds in the world. After building walls to hold back the surf, special machines remove sand and gravel for processing.

The production of salt from sea water is one of the oldest coastal industries. Here salt from a solar plant travels along conveyor belts to the storage area.

confined to shallow, sheltered waters, such as Lake Maracaibo, in Venezuela. Since the early 1950s, however, drilling has been successful in even deeper and more dangerous waters. Floating drilling rigs are used to locate oil and gas deposits, while fixed production platforms are established to extract the fuels.

Production platforms are made of materials that resist corrosion. They are designed to withstand waves more than 20 metres high, together with winds of 240 km/h. Such platforms can now operate in water deeper than 200 metres.

Tourism

Many people spend their annual holiday at the seaside. Coasts are fascinating places because of their wildlife, scenery and opportunities for water sports, such as boating, fishing, swimming, water skiing and wind surfing.

Yet coastal resorts hardly existed before the seventeenth century. However, as travelling became easier in the nineteenth century, more people came to regard coasts as places of pleasure. Most visitors were wealthy and they wanted comfortable places with fine hotels and other services. Gradually, resorts sprang up and many coastal people found work in the growing tourist industry. After the Second World War (1939–45), increased annual holidays and rising incomes caused a new development – more and more people living in cool, rainy countries chose to spend their holidays abroad, where the summers were always hot and dry.

Some coasts, such as that at Torremolinos in southern Spain, have been transformed by tourism.

These yachts are using large, triangular racing sails, called spinnakers, which are designed to give extra speed when sailing with the wind.

In Europe, the countries around the Mediterranean Sea benefited as visitors from northern Europe began to invade their beaches. Spain, a popular destination, received 6,000,000 visitors in 1960. The Spanish government encourages the tourist industry and trains people involved in it, including hotel managers, guides and chefs. The government also supervises the services offered to tourists, trying to ensure that they enjoy themselves. As a result, tourism has become one of Spain's leading industries. By the mid-1980s, Spain was entertaining over 40 million visitors a year, and the tourist industry employed 10 per cent of the Spanish workforce.

The growth of tourism has unfortunate side effects, such as pollution and the construction of ugly buildings on once scenic coasts. However, many magnificent coastlines are now protected for future generations in such sanctuaries as the Pembrokeshire Coast National Park in Wales and the Acadia National Park in Maine, in the USA.

Coastal pollution

People harm coasts in many ways. Poisonous wastes are sometimes poured directly into the sea. Oil tanker accidents and the deliberate release of oil when tankers are cleaned create floating oil slicks which kill wildlife and foul beaches. And some of the detergents used to clean up the oil are also poisonous to many creatures.

Factory waste is a major pollutant, especially near large ports and industrial cities, and it can endanger not only marine life, but also people. For example, from 1953 to 1970, members of fishing families around Minamata Bay, Kyushu island, Japan fell ill with mercury poisoning. More than a hundred people became seriously ill before the cause of the sickness was found. They had eaten fish and shellfish which had absorbed poisons in the industrial wastes.

Pesticides used by farmers also cause pollution. Mixed with particles of soil they are washed into rivers and finally down to the sea. The pesticides poison the water and the soil silts up estuaries. Human and animal wastes also cause problems, as does thermal pollution. This occurs when hot water from nuclear and other power stations is pumped into estuaries or into the sea. This raises the water temperature, with disastrous results for many marine creatures.

Many coastal waters in the Mediterranean Sea, the Sea of Japan, the Baltic Sea and the coastal waters off north-eastern America have been badly polluted. Because the oceans are joined together, currents transport pollutants around the world. Scientists have recently reported that nowhere in the Atlantic and Pacific Oceans is the water free of traces of human pollution, including radioactive particles from nuclear explosions, the pesticide DDT, oil, and mercury from industrial wastes.

The international trade in oil has led to increasing pollution in many coastal areas.

The Nile delta, seen here from space, is now retreating. This is because much of the silt carried by the river now settles on the floor of Lake Nasser, behind the Aswan High Dam. As a result, sea water is spreading inland into farming areas, and the Mediterranean Sea is getting fewer of the nutrients that marine creatures need.

39

Conservation

People are beginning to realize that interference with nature can have far-reaching effects. On a small scale, experts have shown the dangers of 'improving' beaches by removing sand from the lower part and dumping it at the top. The effect is to steepen the slope of the beach and, therefore, to increase the erosive power of the waves. Wave erosion increases in vigour, threatening coastal property. On a global scale, more people understand that the effects of pollution may be felt thousands of kilometres from their source. This has led, for example, to the banning of the use of DDT for most purposes in some countries, including the USA in 1972.

In 1982, the governments of Mediterranean countries signed an agreement to clean up the Mediterranean Sea. They realized that continuing pollution will ultimately threaten tourism.

In many countries attempts are being made to protect coasts. For example, after the Second World War, the population of California grew rapidly. The Pacific coast, which offered desirable places for homes and recreation, was rapidly damaged. About two-thirds of the coastal wetlands and estuaries were destroyed, and sewage, factory wastes and hot water polluted the sea. Mounting concern led the California state legislature to pass a Coastal Act in 1972. Through this Act, many coastal areas threatened with development have been protected, proposed houses have been repositioned to avoid spoiling coastal scenery and wetlands are being restored and conserved.

Everyone who visits coasts can help to conserve them. In many countries, young people are taught to protect nature. The British Nature Conservancy Council has drawn up a Coastal Code, to encourage people to protect wildlife and to avoid killing plants and animals.

The Farne Islands, off the coast of north-eastern England, are a nature reserve owned by the National Trust. Many seabirds, including puffins, nest here.

Above Many young people are keenly aware of the urgent need to conserve nature. Here a team of people has cleared a beach and made a bonfire from the rubbish they have collected.

Below Floating booms are used to contain oil slicks at sea. Around two million tonnes of oil are discharged every year into the oceans, either accidentally or deliberately when oil tankers are cleaned.

New technology

Because oil, natural gas and coal are being used up at such a fast rate, scientists are studying alternative ways of producing electrical energy. Some involve coastal waters.

Tidal power was first harnessed in tide mills around 1,000 years ago. At high tide, water was trapped behind a floodgate. The trapped water was later used to drive a water wheel. Far more sophisticated is the tidal power station opened in 1966 on the estuary of the River Rance, near St Malo in France. It can produce 500,000 kilowatts of electrical power, which is among the cheapest in France. Many other similar stations could be built, though this is unlikely while the cost of energy produced by fossil fuels remains low.

Wave power is another possibility. One system involves the use of floats that contain open, vertical tubes. As waves pass, the water and air in the tubes rise and fall like a piston. The rising air drives air turbines which when linked to generators, produce electricity.

Fish farming is becoming important on some coasts. Breeding oysters and mussels in tanks before moving them to the sea-bed is an ancient industry. Today, fish are also reared and released into rivers, lakes or coastal waters. This technique works well with such fish as salmon, which eventually return to the rivers where they were released when young. But farming most species on a large scale would involve building huge networks of cages on the sea-bed.

Underwater fish farming might be combined with the development of underwater habitats where people could live and work. Experts have also proposed that, as the world's population increases, artificial islands might be built offshore and used as industrial sites or even new towns.

Main picture An artist's impression of future sea floor technology, with fish farms, living habitats, conservatories, robot equipment and various transport systems.

K-3Г

Above The River Rance tidal power station in France.

Inland side

Dam

Road

Water flow

Seaward side

Turbine

Glossary

Arctic Circle   The imaginary circle around the world, parallel to the equator, at latitude 66 32′N.

Attrition   The grinding down of rock particles by water, wind or ice.

Bivalve   An animal enclosed by two hinged, matching shells, such as a clam or oyster.

Calcium carbonate   A chemical substance with the formula $CaCO_3$, which is the main constituent of limestone, chalk, marble and coral.

Delta   A flat area at the mouth of a river made up of river-borne sediment. If offshore currents are strong, they remove the sediment and deltas do not form.

Depression   A low pressure air system associated with unsettled and often stormy weather.

Drifting   A type of fishing employing long, rectangular nets. They are often called gill nets, because the fish are trapped in the nets by their gills.

Echo-sounder   An instrument to measure the depth of the sea or shoals of fish by transmitting sound waves and recording the echoes that are reflected back.

Estuary   The part of a river where it nears the sea. It contains a mixture of fresh river water and salty sea water.

Fossil fuels   Fuels, namely coal, oil and natural gas, formed by the fossilization of once living things.

Glacial valleys   Steep-sided, flat-bottomed valleys worn out by glaciers. They are U-shaped, unlike V-shaped river valleys.

Hydraulic action   Pressure caused by water power.

Industrial Revolution   The period when a country's economy changes and manufacturing becomes dominant. The first country to undergo an Industrial Revolution was Britain in the late eighteenth century.

Invertebrates   Animals without backbones.

Migrants   Animals that move from one region or country to another.

Ocean current   A fast moving flow of water in the oceans. (Drifts are slower currents.)

Predator   An animal that hunts and kills others for food.

Radar   An electronic instrument used in navigation, weather studies, and so on, to locate moving or stationary objects.

Seining   A method of catching fish on the sea-bed, by trapping them in a circular net.

Spawn   To deposit eggs.

Temperate   A moderate, mild climate, between tropical and polar.

Trawling   A type of fishing using bag-shaped nets. They are towed by ships called trawlers.

Left A fortified island off the Greek coast.

Further reading

Many books have been written about the fascinating plants and animals in the sea and on the sea-shore. To find out about the particular species on coasts near your home, you should ask your local librarian to recommend books that describe them. Some useful general books are:

J. Barrett and C.M. Yonge *The Collins Pocket Guide to the Sea Shore* (Collins 1958)

S. Peter Dance *Seashells* (Hamlyn 1971)
I.O. Evans *The Observer's Book of Sea and Seashore* (Warne 1962)
Hans Hvass *Fishes of the World* (Eyre Methuen 1965)
David Saunders *Seabirds* (Hamlyn 1976)
Tony and Hilary Soper *Beside the Sea* (BBC Publications 1979)
J.A. Steers *The Sea Coast* (Collins 1954)

Picture acknowledgements

The author and publishers would like to thank the following for allowing their illustrations to be reproduced in this book: Bryan and Cherry Alexander 4, 15 (top), 27 (top left), 31; De Beers 35 (left); Bruce Coleman Ltd cover (inset), 5, 8, 16, 17, 23, 26, 27 (top right), 29 (top); GeoScience Features cover, 9, 10, 20–21, 30, 38, 41 (bottom); Brian Hawkes 7 (bottom), 40, 41 (top); the Hutchison Library 36; Frank Lane Picture Agency Ltd 11, 14, 15 (bottom), 17, 24, 25 (both), 35 (right); Oxford Scientific Films back cover, 5 (top), 7 (top), 12, 13, 27 (main picture), 28; The Research House 39; John Topham Picture Library 37; ZEFA 34, 43; all other pictures are from the Wayland Picture Library. All illustrations are by Stefan Chabluk.

Index

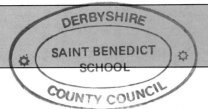